Daddy's Day at the Park

Written by T. L. Wynne
Illustrated by Lisa Reid-Williamson

Daddy's Day at the Park

No part of this publication may be reproduced in whole or in part, or stored in a retrieval system, transmitted in any form or by any means, electronic, mechanical, photocopying, recording, or otherwise, without written permission of the publisher. For more information regarding permission, contact **i am me, LLC**. www.iammeinitiative.com

ISBN-13: 978-0-9987915-2-4   Printed in USA

The Daddy Daughter series is based on the positive relationship between a father and his young daughter. Exuding the importance of a father's influence in his daughter's life, illustrating their relationship and exciting adventures together.

Daddy and Me
available now at
www.iammeinitiative.com

Everyday you remind me of the importance of time spent with the ones who make life worthwhile.

-Dad

The sun was shining, and the birds were chirping.

"Can we please have pancakes and orange juice?"

"You go and get ready, and I'll see what I can do."

"Well let's get in the car and go.. go .. go!"

It goes up and down and round and round, it was one of Amiyah's favorite rides.

"Let's go to the swings I see my friends!"

They screamed "OHH OHH AHH AHH", chasing one another.

"I packed your favorite peanut butter and jelly."
"1 for you and 2 for me."

"I had a great day Daddy, this was so much fun."

"So did I princess, and best of all I spent it with my favorite little one."

www.ingramcontent.com/pod-product-compliance
Lightning Source LLC
Chambersburg PA
CBHW051555010526
44118CB00022B/2720